101
QUIZZES
FOR
COUPLES

101
QUIZZES
FOR
COUPLES

Take these tests to find out who really knows who!

NATASHA BURTON

ADAMS MEDIA

NEW YORK   LONDON   TORONTO   SYDNEY   NEW DELHI

Aadamsmedia

Adams Media
An Imprint of Simon & Schuster, Inc.
57 Littlefield Street
Avon, Massachusetts 02322

For information about special discounts for bulk purchases, please contact Simon & Schuster Special Sales at 1-866-506-1949 or business@simonandschuster.com.

The Simon & Schuster Speakers Bureau can bring authors to your live event. For more information or to book an event contact the Simon & Schuster Speakers Bureau at 1-866-248-3049 or visit our website at www.simonspeakers.com.

Manufactured in the United States of America

20 19 18 17 16 15 14 13 12

ISBN 978-1-4405-6742-1
ISBN 978-1-4405-6743-8 (ebook)

DEDICATION
For Greg

CONTENTS

ACKNOWLEDGMENTS

I WOULD LIKE TO THANK the team at Adams Media, specifically Halli Melnitsky, for entrusting me with this project, Peter Archer, my patient and skillful editor, and Brendan O'Neill for his continued support of my writing. On that same note, I am forever grateful to my wonderful agent, Elizabeth Evans, and the team at Jean V. Naggar Literary Agency for guiding me through my career.

Writing about relationships requires research, which often comes in the form of asking people personal questions about their lives, and hoping they're willing to respond. To this end, I am very appreciative of those who volunteered their invaluable insight for this book: Alison Singh Gee, Eric Jones, Kim Fay, Brienne Walsh, Justin Veschi, Carrie Price, Lorena O'Neil, Julie Holop, Brett Smiley, Akira Okubo, Nene Crawford, Carly Paris, Noelle Sprunger, Megan Isennock, Taylor Way, Emily Levy, Ganene Valencia, and Mike Mussack. Thank you.

Also instrumental in this process are my lifelong best friends, Jennifer Jacobson, Alana Aranki, and Ciji Saso, as well as their lovely husbands, for their support and suggestions. I am also indebted to my (four!) incredibly encouraging parents, Manny and Tania Francisco, and Dan and Wendy Burton.

But, above all, I would like to thank the love of my life, my fiancé Greg St. Clair, for being my constant inspiration. It's an honor to be able to write about relationships while being as happy as you've made me.

INTRODUCTION

Whether you've been together for three months, three years, or three decades, there's always something new to learn about your partner, like:

- What's his favorite movie of all time?
- What famous person from the past would she like to invite to dinner?
- What was his special childhood secret place?
- What makes her laugh until she can't breathe?

The exciting thing about relationships at any stage is there's always a new, undiscovered horizon waiting for you to explore. That's what the quizzes in this book will help you to do.

Of course, you may be thinking, "But I already know everything about my partner." Rest assured, there's always something new to discover. With this book to help you, you'll get into the hows, whys, and whens of each other's idiosyncrasies. If you're just starting out as a couple, you'll learn how to make your relationship deeper and more caring. If you've been together for years, these quizzes will spark that connection you had when you first started dating.

There are few periods of life more thrilling than this beginning. The potent cocktail of being loved and being in love (and, let's be honest, in lust) makes every discovery about your partner feel monumental.

You spend hours learning new facts about each other, hearing each other's childhood stories for the first time, and swapping secrets about your pasts. You're so eager to sponge up every detail that you might even start Googling your beloved just to get one more ounce of info.

That's the feeling these quizzes will bring to you. It's fun to find out what each of you wants out of a vacation, or what kind of television show you'd each create, given the chance. This book will give you insight into each other when you talk about what's the most important thing in a relationship, or how much (or little) you enjoy spending time with other people. With each answer, you'll want to know more.

Because this book aims to provide meaningful conversation for a wide range of couples, some questions may not apply to you or your relationship. But rather than skip them, be creative and tailor those rare instances to your particular situation.

HOW TO USE THIS BOOK

There's no right (or wrong) way to use this book. You could choose to tackle a quiz every day, or hunker down and go through all of them in one sitting. (If that's the route you take, though, you may want to open a bottle of wine first.)

However you choose to take these quizzes, find a setting and medium that works for you and your relationship. After all, these conversations don't have to happen face-to-face in your bedroom or living room.

Perhaps you could store this book in your glove box, so you can do the quizzes on your next car trip or trek down to the in-laws. Long-distance couples might use this book as a way to bond from afar, going through the quizzes over video chat, on the phone, or through e-mail. Anything goes!

ABOUT THE QUIZZES

Each page of this book is designed to spark lively debate or thought-provoking conversation with quizzes that range from serious to silly to sexy. Here are the various types you'll find:

INTERVIEW

These quizzes are a straightforward series of questions for each of you to answer. (You'll also see some quickie interviews, which are designed to be more rapid-fire, and should require less thought to answer.)

THIS OR THAT? and WOULD YOU RATHER?

Here, you'll choose what you like best (or what you'd prefer) from a series of "either-or" questions to see how you and your partner match up.

CHECKLIST

This quiz provides an already-made list, on which you and your partner will check off each of your preferences.

MULTIPLE CHOICE

Each question in these quizzes presents some options to get the conversation going. However, these choices should by no means limit you. The options are designed to get you thinking, but there may be more possibilities between them.

WHO DOES IT BETTER?

It's you versus your partner in these quizzes, for which you have to decide who is more skilled at certain tasks (or would fare better in hypothetical situations).

LAST WORD

While this is a book of "quizzes," it's not about the right answers—or having the same answers, for that matter. Rather, insert text about the one you love most. So, without further ado, grab your partner and ask away!

101
QUIZZES
FOR
COUPLES

YOUR FIRSTS

1. When, where, and with whom was your first kiss?

_____

_____

2. Who did you have your first crush on?

_____

_____

3. What was the first thing in life that broke your heart?

_____

_____

4. What's your first memory?

_____

_____

5. What was your first pet?

_____

_____

6. What's the first word you said?

_____

_____

7. Who was your first friend?

_____

_____

8. What was the first really big-time injury you incurred?

_____

_____

9. What was the first book you remember reading?

_____

_____

10. What was the first huge thing you accomplished in life? (Or, at least, the first thing you thought was huge.)

_____

_____

WHAT INSPIRES YOU?

1. Do you have a favorite quote or words by which to live?

_____

_____

2. Who's the person you admire most (someone you actually know)?

_____

_____

3. Who's the person you admire most (someone who's a public figure)?

_____

_____

4. Where does your drive come from?

_____

_____

5. Do you consider yourself an ambitious person?

_____

_____

6. Has what inspires you changed over time?

_____

_____

7. Do you feel you're more or less ambitious now than when you were younger?

_____

_____

8. How do you stay motivated when you've had a setback?

_____

_____

9. How can I inspire you to stay driven or motivated?

_____

_____

10. Is there anything I do that inhibits your drive or makes you feel less motivated?

_____

_____

OTHER PEOPLE'S RELATIONSHIPS

1. Which of your friends' relationships do you admire the most?

    _____

    _____

2. Which of your friends do you think is the most likely to be unfaithful to his/her partner?

    _____

    _____

3. Which of your friends do you see getting divorced someday?

    _____

    _____

4. Which of your friends do you see never marrying?

    _____

    _____

5. Which of your friends would be the best parents?

    _____

    _____

6. Which of your friends would be the worst parents?

    _____

    _____

7. What have you learned from watching your friends' relationships progress over the years?

_____

_____

8. How have your friends helped you in your relationships?

_____

_____

9. Which friend would you turn to first for advice if we were having problems?

_____

_____

10. What advice would you give a friend who is having problems in his/her relationship?

_____

_____

_____

_____

WHICH POP CULTURE REFERENCE DO YOU LIKE MORE?

Friends or *Seinfeld*?   Me _____ You _____

Star Trek or Star Wars?   Me _____ You _____

'80s fashion or '90s fashion?   Me _____ You _____

Nickelodeon or Disney Channel?   Me _____ You _____

Disneyland or Disney World?   Me _____ You _____

The Simpsons or *Family Guy*?   Me _____ You _____

Sleepaway camp or day camp?   Me _____ You _____

Boy Meets World or *Full House*?   Me _____ You _____

Kool-Aid or Capri Sun?   Me _____ You _____

The Muppet Show or *Fraggle Rock*?   Me _____ You _____

Coke or Pepsi?   Me _____ You _____

LA Gears or Airwalks?   Me _____ You _____

Nintendo or Xbox?   Me _____ You _____

WHAT ADVICE WOULD YOU GIVE TO YOUR PAST SELF, IF YOU HAD THE CHANCE?

1. As a little kid?

_____

_____

_____

_____

2. During puberty?

_____

_____

_____

_____

3. When you were a freshman in high school?

_____

_____

_____

_____

4. On prom night?

_____

_____

_____

_____

5. When you didn't want to listen to your parents as a teenager?

_____

_____

6. While you were applying to college?

_____

_____

_____

7. When you were out partying in college?

_____

_____

_____

8. At college graduation?

_____

_____

_____

9. After your first heartbreak?

_____

_____

_____

10. When you got your first job?

_____

_____

_____

HOW MANY OF THESE BODY ODDITIES CAN YOU DO?

Touch your tongue to your nose   **Me** ❏ | **You** ❏

Touch your tongue to your chin   **Me** ❏ | **You** ❏

Raise one eyebrow   **Me** ❏ | **You** ❏

Lick your elbow   **Me** ❏ | **You** ❏

Roll your tongue like a wave   **Me** ❏ | **You** ❏

Curl the sides of your tongue up   **Me** ❏ | **You** ❏

Wiggle your nose   **Me** ❏ | **You** ❏

Bend your thumb to your forearm   **Me** ❏ | **You** ❏

Put your whole fist in your mouth   **Me** ❏ | **You** ❏

Go cross-eyed   **Me** ❏ | **You** ❏

Wiggle your ears   **Me** ❏ | **You** ❏

HOW WOULD WE
DESCRIBE US?

1. Happy-go-lucky or cynical? **Me** _____ **You** _____

2. Cat or dog person? **Me** _____ **You** _____

3. More logical or more emotional? **Me** _____ **You** _____

4. Objective or subjective? **Me** _____ **You** _____

5. Friendly or aloof? **Me** _____ **You** _____

6. Spontaneous or careful? **Me** _____ **You** _____

7. Wound up or relaxed? **Me** _____ **You** _____

8. Go-getting or go-with-the-flow? **Me** _____ **You** _____

9. Gullible or skeptical? **Me** _____ **You** _____

10. Confident or second-guessing? **Me** _____ **You** _____

OUR SEX LIFE

1. How do you feel about the number of times we have sex each week?
Too much / Not enough / Just right

2. How do you feel about our level of role-playing?
Too much / Not enough / Just right

3. How do you feel about how much lingerie is worn?
Too much / Not enough / Just right

4. How do you feel about the frequency of oral sex we have?
Too much / Not enough / Just right

5. How's my level of general, everyday affection toward you?
Too much / Not enough / Just right

6. How do you feel about how often I give you massages?
Too much / Not enough / Just right

7. How are we doing with trying new things sexually in general?
Too much / Not enough / Just right

8. How's our level of experimenting with different positions?
Too much / Not enough / Just right

9. How do you feel about how often you initiate sex?
Too much / Not enough / Just right

10. How do you feel about how often I initiate sex?
Too much / Not enough / Just right

WHAT'S YOUR FOOD PREFERENCE?

Hot dog or hamburger?   Me _____   You _____

Omelet or scrambled?   Me _____   You _____

Mild or spicy?   Me _____   You _____

Sushi or sashimi?   Me _____   You _____

Coke or Pepsi?   Me _____   You _____

Oatmeal or cereal?   Me _____   You _____

Ham or bacon?   Me _____   You _____

Apple or orange?   Me _____   You _____

Salsa or guacamole?   Me _____   You _____

Ketchup or mustard?   Me _____   You _____

Yellow or spicy mustard?   Me _____   You _____

Ice cream or frozen yogurt?   Me _____   You _____

Coleslaw or potato salad?   Me _____   You _____

Peach or nectarine?   Me _____   You _____

Pancakes or waffles?   Me _____   You _____

Taco or burrito?   Me _____   You _____

MORE
OF YOUR FIRSTS

1. What was the first concert you ever went to?

   _____

   _____

   _____

2. When was the first time you failed at something?

   _____

   _____

   _____

3. When was the first time you stood up to someone?

   _____

   _____

   _____

4. When was the first time you ever went to a hospital?

   _____

   _____

   _____

5. When was the first time you went to a wedding?

   _____

   _____

   _____

6. When was the first time you went to a funeral?

_____

_____

_____

7. When was your first time being away from home?

_____

_____

_____

8. Where and when was your first sleepover?

_____

_____

_____

9. When was your first realization your parents were human (i.e., not perfect)?

_____

_____

_____

10. When did you get your first cell phone?

_____

_____

_____

A FEW OF YOUR FAVORITE THINGS

1. Favorite color?

   Me _____ **You** _____

2. Favorite scent?

   Me _____ **You** _____

3. Favorite place on Earth?

   Me _____ **You** _____

4. Favorite day of the week?

   Me _____ **You** _____

5. Favorite dessert?

   Me _____ **You** _____

6. Favorite book?

   Me _____ **You** _____

7. Favorite song?

   Me _____ **You** _____

8. Favorite movie?

   Me _____ **You** _____

9. Favorite possession?

   Me _____ **You** _____

10. Favorite thing to do on a Friday night?

    Me _____ **You** _____

11. Favorite thing to do on a Sunday night?

    Me _____ **You** _____

12. Favorite piece of art?

    Me _____ **You** _____

13. Favorite candy?

    Me _____ **You** _____

14. Favorite toy from childhood?

    Me _____ **You** _____

15. Favorite spot in your home?

    Me _____ **You** _____

16. Favorite time of day?

    Me _____ **You** _____

OMG
WE'RE GOING TO TALK ABOUT BECOMING PARENTS NOW

1. What are your thoughts on becoming a parent someday?

_____

_____

_____

2. Do you have an ideal age when you would like to have kids?

_____

_____

_____

3. How many kids would you like to have?

_____

_____

_____

4. What's the one thing you don't want to do as a parent?

_____

_____

_____

5. What's the biggest mistake you think your parents made raising you?

_____

_____

_____

6. What's your biggest fear about becoming a parent?

_____

_____

_____

7. Is there anything you're looking forward to about having kids?

_____

_____

_____

8. Do you have a preference in terms of having a girl or a boy?

_____

_____

_____

9. How do you think a couple's relationship changes when they have children?

_____

_____

_____

10. What do you think is the most important thing to take into consideration before starting a family?

_____

_____

_____

YOUR PAST LOVERS

1. How many significant relationships have you had?

_____

_____

_____

2. Have you ever been dumped?

_____

_____

_____

3. Have you ever dumped someone?

_____

_____

_____

4. What's the craziest thing you ever did for love?

_____

_____

_____

5. How often do you talk to your exes?

_____

_____

_____

6. What's your biggest relationship regret?

_____

_____

_____

7. What's the worst thing a former lover has ever done to you?

_____

_____

_____

8. What was your go-to pickup line or tactic for hitting on someone?

_____

_____

_____

9. Has someone you loved ever broken your trust?

_____

_____

_____

10. Have you ever been cheated on?

_____

_____

_____

11. Have you ever cheated?

_____

_____

_____

12. How has your definition of love changed over time?

_____

_____

_____

13. To whom have you said, "I love you"?

_____

_____

_____

14. What's the most embarrassing thing you've ever done in a relationship?

_____

_____

_____

You □ Me
You □ Me
You □ Me
You □ Me
You □ Me
You □ Me
You □ Me
You □ Me

YOUR RELATIONSHIP
PHILOSOPHIES AND GOALS

1. What do you think is the role or purpose of a romantic relationship?

_____

_____

_____

2. Do you believe in the institution of marriage?

_____

_____

_____

3. Do you think that making a lifelong commitment is realistic?

_____

_____

_____

4. To what extent do you expect our relationship to last?

_____

_____

_____

5. Do you think two people ever really know each other completely?

_____

_____

_____

WOULD YOU RATHER?

Skydive or bungee jump? * Become president or become r

something that changes the world or win the lottery? * Cl

Mount Everest or scuba-dive the Great Blue Hole in Beli

* Publish a bestselling book or write a hit song? * Go to C

nival in Rio or do running with the bulls in Spain? * Join

6. How long do you think two people should date before getting married?

_____

7. To what extent should each member of a couple maintain his/her own independence?

_____

_____

_____

8. When you were younger, what were your relationship goals?

_____

_____

_____

9. How have these goals changed over the years?

_____

_____

_____

10. What do you think our relationship adds to your life?

_____

_____

_____

WHO DOES STUFF AROUND THE HOUSE BETTER?
(TREAD LIGHTLY OR YOU MAY GET MORE CHORES . . .)

1. Washes dishes   Me _____ You _____

2. Folds the laundry   Me _____ You _____

3. Cooks dinner   Me _____ You _____

4. Cleans the bathroom   Me _____ You _____

5. Shops for groceries   Me _____ You _____

6. Mows the lawn   Me _____ You _____

7. Makes the bed   Me _____ You _____

8. Cooks breakfast   Me _____ You _____

9. Makes coffee   Me _____ You _____

10. Hosts guests   Me _____ You _____

11. Fixes things   Me _____ You _____

12. Controls the TV remote   Me _____ You _____

YOUR FRIENDSHIPS

1. Who do you consider your closest friend?

_____

_____

_____

2. What do you think is the most essential part of a friendship?

_____

_____

_____

3. What role do your friendships play in your life?

_____

_____

_____

4. Which of your friends can you depend on most in case of a crisis?

_____

_____

_____

5. Which of your friends is most likely to get you into trouble?

_____

_____

_____

6. How have your friendships changed as you've aged?

7. How have your friendships changed since we began our relationship?

8. What qualities do you look for in a friend?

9. How do your relationships with members of the opposite sex differ from your same-sex friendships?

10. How close do you think people should be with their opposite-sex friends when they're in relationships? (As in, where is the line?)

11. Do you look at your friendships as an extension of your family? If no, why not?

WHO WOULD YOU WANNA BE?

A crazy-good athlete or a superhero?   Me _____ You _____

A supermodel or a genius?   Me _____ You _____

A respected millionaire or
a despised billionaire?   Me _____ You _____

A genie who gives wishes or
a wish receiver?   Me _____ You _____

A pop star or a rock star?   Me _____ You _____

The president or royalty?   Me _____ You _____

The Pope or the Dalai Lama?   Me _____ You _____

A nightly news anchor or
a soap opera star?   Me _____ You _____

A chess champion or
a Rubik's Cube record–breaker?   Me _____ You _____

A high-profile movie star or
a lesser-known TV actor?   Me _____ You _____

BLENDING OUR FAMILIES

1. What's your overall impression of my family?

2. Who do you connect with best?

3. How do you see yourself fitting in with my family?

4. How often do you think we should visit our families?

5. How do you feel about sharing holidays with our families, or would you prefer to switch off?

6. How do you think our families would interact with one another?

_____

7. Is there anyone in your family or mine whom you wouldn't want around our children?

_____

_____

_____

8. Who would you want to take care of our kids should something happen to us?

_____

_____

_____

9. Who do you think I would get along best with from your family?

_____

_____

_____

10. Who do you think I would butt heads with the most in your family?

_____

_____

_____

WHEN'S THE LAST TIME YOU...

1. Laughed until you cried?

_____

_____

_____

2. Cried-cried?

_____

_____

_____

3. Felt let down by someone?

_____

_____

_____

4. Felt disappointed in yourself?

_____

_____

_____

5. Did something you regretted?

_____

_____

_____

6. Felt proud of yourself?

_____

_____

_____

7. Totally embarrassed yourself?

_____

_____

_____

8. Screwed something up really badly?

_____

_____

_____

9. Got so excited about something that you literally jumped for joy?

_____

_____

_____

10. Overreacted about something?

_____

_____

_____

HOW WOULD WE DESCRIBE US?

1. Optimist or pessimist?   Me _____ You _____

2. Extrovert or introvert?   Me _____ You _____

3. Outgoing or shy?   Me _____ You _____

4. Logical or emotional?   Me _____ You _____

5. Right-brained or left-brained? Me _____ You _____

6. Book-smart or street-smart?   Me _____ You _____

7. Friendly or standoffish?   Me _____ You _____

8. Impulsive or restrained?   Me _____ You _____

9. Wound up or laid-back?   Me _____ You _____

10. Adventurous or cautious?   Me _____ You _____

WHAT WOULD
YOU DO?

1. If you witnessed someone getting bullied would you . . .
   Step in? / Mind your own business? / Get help?

2. If you found money on the ground would you . . .
   Keep it? / Try to find the owner? / Depends on how much money

3. If you overheard that a coworker was about to get fired would you . . .
   Tell him or her?
   Pretend you didn't hear anything?
   Talk to your boss about it?

4. If you knew you had one week to live would you . . .
   Tell your loved ones?
   Keep it to yourself?
   Tell everyone except for _____

5. If you made a big mistake at work—but no one knew you were at fault—would you . . .
   Fess up?
   Stay mum?
   Write an anonymous note saying you're sorry?

6. If you found out that your boss was embezzling money would you . . .
   Report him/her to the authorities?
   Keep the information to yourself?
   Tell someone at the company?

7. If you found a stray dog on your way home—no tags—would you . . .
Take him home? / Leave him be? / Take him to an animal shelter?

8. If you encountered a really intoxicated person at a party would you . . .
Drive him or her home?
Help the person find his/her friends?
Leave the person alone?

9. If you were at a bank while it was being robbed, would you . . .
Try to stop the perpetrators?
Just follow the robber's instructions?
Attempt to covertly alert the authorities?

10. If one of your friends had a really bad hygiene problem would you . . .
Be direct and tell him/her?
Say nothing?
Write the person an anonymous note?

11. If you knew a friend's significant other was cheating on him/her would you . . .
Tell the friend?
Keep out of it?
Confront his/her significant other?

12. If you knew your friend was cheating on his/her significant other would you . . .
Encourage him/her to stop?
Stay out of it?
Stop being friends with him/her?

13. If you saw a woman being assaulted, would you . . .
Step in?
Mind your own business?
Get help?

WHICH HISTORICAL FIGURE WOULD YOU WANNA GRAB A DRINK WITH?

1. Albert Einstein
   or Benjamin Franklin?   Me _____ You _____

2. Joan of Arc or Amelia Earhart?   Me _____ You _____

3. Jane Austen or Virginia Woolf?   Me _____ You _____

4. Kurt Cobain or Jimi Hendrix?   Me _____ You _____

5. Sigmund Freud or Alfred Kinsey?   Me _____ You _____

6. Galileo Galilei or Socrates?   Me _____ You _____

7. Henry Ford or Thomas Edison?   Me _____ You _____

8. Abraham Lincoln
   or John F. Kennedy?   Me _____ You _____

9. Marilyn Monroe
   or Audrey Hepburn?   Me _____ You _____

10. Mahatma Gandhi
    or Mother Teresa?   Me _____ You _____

11. Martin Luther King Jr.
    or Moses?   Me _____ You _____

12. Leonardo da Vinci
    or Pablo Picasso?   Me _____ You _____

13. Charles Darwin
    or Sir Isaac Newton?   Me _____ You _____

LET'S TALK ABOUT SEX, BABY

1. Who's the first person to whom you were sexually attracted?

_____

_____

_____

2. How has what you're attracted to sexually changed over time?

_____

_____

_____

3. What do you remember about the first time you had sex?

_____

_____

_____

4. How would you describe your sex drive?

_____

_____

_____

5. Is there anything sexual or sex-related that weirds you out?

_____

_____

_____

6. How did you learn about what to do during sex?

_____

_____

_____

7. How has the quality of your sexual experience changed over the years?

_____

_____

_____

8. How do you feel about masturbation?

_____

_____

_____

9. How do you feel about using toys or props during sex?

_____

_____

_____

10. Is there anything sexual that you absolutely will never try?

_____

_____

_____

11. How long would it typically take for you to date someone before sleeping with him/her?

_____

_____

_____

SPLITSVILLE

1. How do you feel about divorce?

_____
_____
_____

2. Why do you think the divorce rate is so high these days?

_____
_____
_____

3. Do you have a history of divorce in your family?

_____
_____
_____

4. Do you think people who have witnessed divorce are more inclined to divorce themselves?

_____
_____
_____

5. Should couples enter into marriage realistically, thinking that they might divorce some day, or steadfastly believe it will never be a viable option?

_____
_____
_____

6. How long would you be willing to work on a marriage before resorting to divorce?

_____

_____

7. Under what circumstances (if any) would the only possible outcome for your marriage be divorce?

_____

_____

_____

8. Would having children change your viewpoint on divorce in any way?

_____

_____

_____

9. In what situations (if any) do you think having divorced parents could be better for children?

_____

_____

_____

10. In what ways do you think you've been affected by divorce, either personally or tangentially?

_____

_____

_____

THINGS YOU WANT
IN A VACATION

Relaxing on a beach	Me ❑	You ❑
Shopping	Me ❑	You ❑
Hitting up all of the main attractions	Me ❑	You ❑
Nightlife	Me ❑	You ❑
Schedule of activities planned in advance	Me ❑	You ❑
Ability to see the indigenous people and how they live	Me ❑	You ❑
An all-inclusive resort with a pool	Me ❑	You ❑
Adventure—like hiking, zip-lining, or kayaking	Me ❑	You ❑
Fruity, blended cocktails	Me ❑	You ❑
A spa treatment (or two)	Me ❑	You ❑
Tours of historical landmarks	Me ❑	You ❑
No-frills accommodations	Me ❑	You ❑
A cute little town to check out	Me ❑	You ❑

Skydive or bungee jump? * Become president or become [...] something that changes the world or win the lottery? * [...] * Publish a bestselling book or write a hit song? * Go to [...]

A day or two to do absolutely nothing	Me ❑	You ❑
Sun and warm temperatures	Me ❑	You ❑
Playing sports like golf or tennis	Me ❑	You ❑
Being able to go swimming	Me ❑	You ❑
Cold weather and snow	Me ❑	You ❑
Seclusion	Me ❑	You ❑

WHAT'S YOUR STANCE ON THESE DATING "RULES"?

1. The man should always pay for the first date.
   Agree because ... Disagree because ... Depends because ...

   _____

   _____

   _____

   _____

2. If a guy texts a woman, instead of calls, he's not that into her.
   Agree because ... Disagree because ... Depends because ...

   _____

   _____

   _____

   _____

3. Don't play games.
   Agree because ... Disagree because ... Depends because ...

   _____

   _____

   _____

   _____

4. A woman should wait for the guy to call after the first date.
   Agree because ... Disagree because ... Depends because ...

   _____

   _____

   _____

5. If a woman is into a guy, she shouldn't make herself too available.
   Agree because ... Disagree because ... Depends because ...

6. Don't sleep with someone too soon.
   Agree because ... Disagree because ... Depends because ...

7. The guy should say "I love you" before the woman.
   Agree because ... Disagree because ... Depends because ...

8. Don't waste time on someone you're not sexually compatible with.
   Agree because ... Disagree because ... Depends because ...

9. A woman should wait for the guy to bring up defining the relationship, marriage, and so on.
   Agree because ... Disagree because ... Depends because ...

10. You should wait until marriage to move in together.
    Agree because ... Disagree because ... Depends because ...

HOW ABOUT SOME IN-DEPTH SEX TALK?

1. What do you think is the best thing about our sex life?

_____

_____

2. What would you change about our sex life?

_____

_____

3. What are you most self-conscious about in bed?

_____

_____

4. What do you think I'm self-conscious about?

_____

_____

5. What's your favorite "move" of mine?

_____

_____

6. What's your favorite thing to do in bed?

_____

_____

WOULD YOU RATHER?

Skydive or bungee jump? * Become president or become ...

Mount Everest or scuba-dive the Great Blue Hole in Bel...

* Publish a bestselling book or write a hit song? * Go to ...

7. Is there anything I do to you, sexually, that you don't like?

_____

_____

_____

8. How do you think our sex life affects our relationship?

_____

_____

_____

9. How would our relationship be affected if one of us lost his/her desire for sex?

_____

_____

_____

10. What's the ideal time of day to have sex?

_____

_____

_____

11. Where's your favorite place to have sex?

_____

_____

_____

12. How often do you feel satisfied in bed?

_____

_____

_____

WHAT MAKES YOU LAUGH?

1. How would you describe your sense of humor?

_____

_____

_____

2. What's the corniest joke you've ever heard?

_____

_____

_____

3. What's the dirtiest joke you've ever heard?

_____

_____

_____

4. Who is your favorite standup comedian?

_____

_____

_____

5. From where do you get your sense of humor?

_____

_____

_____

6. What's your favorite funny movie?

_____

_____

_____

7. What's your favorite sitcom?

_____

_____

_____

8. What kinds of jokes or humor do you find totally not funny?

_____

_____

_____

9. Who is your funniest friend or family member?

_____

_____

_____

10. When you need cheering up, what always makes you laugh?

_____

_____

_____

WHO WOULD YOU RATHER
HAVE DINNER WITH?

Barack Obama or Michelle Obama? **Me** _____ **You** _____

George W. Bush or George H.W. Bush? **Me** _____ **You** _____

Bill Clinton or Hillary Clinton? **Me** _____ **You** _____

Michael Jordan or Charles Barkley? **Me** _____ **You** _____

Peyton Manning or John Elway? **Me** _____ **You** _____

Steven Tyler or Mick Jagger? **Me** _____ **You** _____

Warren Buffett or Bill Gates? **Me** _____ **You** _____

Stephen Colbert or Jon Stewart? **Me** _____ **You** _____

Bill O'Reilly or Glenn Beck? **Me** _____ **You** _____

Mark Zuckerberg or Al Gore? **Me** _____ **You** _____

Adele or Lady Gaga? **Me** _____ **You** _____

Angelina Jolie or Jennifer Aniston? **Me** _____ **You** _____

COMMON CHARACTERISTICS
(PART 1)

1. Who's more logical?   **Me** ❑ ‖ **You** ❑

2. Who's funnier?   **Me** ❑ ‖ **You** ❑

3. Who's more sensitive?   **Me** ❑ ‖ **You** ❑

4. Who's better under pressure?   **Me** ❑ ‖ **You** ❑

5. Who's better dressed?   **Me** ❑ ‖ **You** ❑

6. Who's quicker to anger?   **Me** ❑ ‖ **You** ❑

7. Who's sillier?   **Me** ❑ ‖ **You** ❑

8. Who's better at entertaining him- or herself?   **Me** ❑ ‖ **You** ❑

9. Who's more optimistic?   **Me** ❑ ‖ **You** ❑

10. Who's more ambitious?   **Me** ❑ ‖ **You** ❑

11. Who's more passionate?   **Me** ❑ ‖ **You** ❑

12. Who's more impatient?   **Me** ❑ ‖ **You** ❑

13. Who's friendlier?　　　　　　　　**Me** ❏ ‖ **You** ❏

14. Who gets scared more easily?　　　**Me** ❏ ‖ **You** ❏

15. Who gets jealous more easily?　　　**Me** ❏ ‖ **You** ❏

HOW ANNOYING ARE THESE COMMON PET PEEVES? (PART 1)

1. People who leave the toilet seat up
   Very / A little / Not at all

2. People who smack their gum
   Very / A little / Not at all

3. People who send e-mails with misspellings or bad grammar
   Very / A little / Not at all

4. People who whistle in public
   Very / A little / Not at all

5. People who forget to say "thank you"
   Very / A little / Not at all

6. People who don't use a turn signal
   Very / A little / Not at all

7. People who will tease a dog through a fence
   Very / A little / Not at all

8. People who sit next to you on public transportation even when there are other seats available
Very / A little / Not at all

9. People who text while you're trying to talk to them
Very / A little / Not at all

10. People who restlessly shake their leg
Very / A little / Not at all

THE SPACE-TIME CONTINUUM

1. If you could stay one age forever, what would it be?

_____

_____

_____

2. If you could live in any time period, which would you choose?

_____

_____

_____

3. If you could go back to one day in history, which day would it be?

_____

_____

_____

4. If you could live as anyone else for a day, who would it be?

_____

_____

_____

5. If you could go back to one day of your life and change something, what would you change?

_____

_____

_____

6. If you could visit one point in the future, how far ahead would you go?

_____

7. If you could go back to apologize to someone, who would it be?

_____

_____

_____

8. If you had to live one day over and over and over again, forever, which would it be?

_____

_____

_____

9. What age or year would you least like to go back to?

_____

_____

_____

10. If you had to become an animal or other nonhuman living thing for the rest of your life, what would it be?

_____

_____

_____

HOW WOULD YOU EXPLAIN THE FOLLOWING TO YOUR KIDS?

1. Love?

_____

_____

_____

_____

2. Sex?

_____

_____

_____

_____

3. Death?

_____

_____

_____

_____

4. Violence in the world?

_____

_____

_____

_____

WOULD YOU RATHER?

5. Cancer?

6. Corruption by people in power?

7. God?

8. Drugs and alcohol use?

9. Conflict between us?

10. Strangers?

_____

_____

_____

_____

11. Poverty?

_____

_____

_____

_____

12. Santa Claus?

_____

_____

_____

_____

WHAT ARE YOUR FINANCIAL PRIORITIES?

Buy a house   **Me** ❏ | **You** ❏

Buy a boat   **Me** ❏ | **You** ❏

Pay for our kids' college educations   **Me** ❏ | **You** ❏

Help our parents out when they get old   **Me** ❏ | **You** ❏

Save up for a big vacation   **Me** ❏ | **You** ❏

Save enough to retire early   **Me** ❏ | **You** ❏

Make enough money so we can afford
to shop at an upscale grocery store   **Me** ❏ | **You** ❏

Start a charity for those in need   **Me** ❏ | **You** ❏

Donate money to our alma maters   **Me** ❏ | **You** ❏

Invest in a vacation property   **Me** ❏ | **You** ❏

Give a little money each month to
a cause we care about   **Me** ❏ | **You** ❏

Sponsor an animal   **Me** ❑   │   **You** ❑

Spend money when we feel like it
without having to worry   **Me** ❑   │   **You** ❑

Become debt-free   **Me** ❑   │   **You** ❑

IT'S ALL IN THE FAMILY

1. How did you get along with your parents when you were younger?

_____

_____

_____

2. What qualities do you think you got from your parents?

_____

_____

_____

3. What did you and your parents fight about most when you were growing up?

_____

_____

_____

4. What's your relationship with your siblings like today? Best friends? Never speak to each other? Something in-between?

_____

_____

_____

5. What qualities of your family do you want your own family to have someday?

_____

_____

_____

6. What was the house or apartment you grew up in like?

_____

_____

7. What was the absolute coolest family vacation you took when you were a kid?

_____

_____

_____

8. To which family member are you closest?

_____

_____

_____

9. Who is the weirdest person in your family?

_____

_____

_____

10. What's the most embarrassing story your family loves to tell about you?

_____

_____

_____

11. What's the most embarrassing story you love to tell about someone else in your family?

_____

_____

_____

12. What are some negative things about the way your family behaves?

_____

_____

_____

13. What's your most cherished family tradition?

_____

_____

_____

14. How often do you talk with people in your family?

_____

_____

_____

WHAT WERE YOU LIKE AS A KID?

1. How often did you get put on time-out?
    Sometimes / All the time / Never

2. Were you picked on at school?
    Sometimes / All the time / Never

3. Did you like to play make-believe?
    Sometimes / All the time / Never

4. Would you ever kill bugs for fun?
    Sometimes / All the time / Never

5. Did monsters live in your closet or under your bed?
    Sometimes / All the time / Never

6. Were you a troublemaker in school?
    Sometimes / All the time / Never

7. Did you ever run away from home (or pretend to)?
    Sometimes / All the time / Never

8. Did you ever break curfew?
    Sometimes / All the time / Never

9. Did you talk to an imaginary friend?
   Sometimes / All the time / Never

10. Did you sleep with a stuffed animal?
    Sometimes / All the time / Never

11. Were you interested in the opposite sex?
    Sometimes / All the time / Never

12. Did you get hurt a lot from self-inflicted bodily injuries
    (like from trying to do stunts on your bike)?
    Sometimes / All the time / Never

LOVING THYSELF

1. Who's opinion of you matters the most?

_____

_____

_____

2. Is there a person in your life whom you'd least like to disappoint?

_____

_____

_____

3. In what ways are you too hard on yourself?

_____

_____

_____

4. How would you describe your current state of self-esteem?

_____

_____

_____

5. How has your confidence in yourself changed over time?

_____

_____

_____

6. What most influences your self-esteem?

_____

_____

_____

7. What makes you feel the worst about yourself (like a certain person, habit, or vice)?

_____

_____

_____

8. How does our relationship help your self-esteem?

_____

_____

_____

9. Do I do anything that hurts your confidence?

_____

_____

_____

10. Is there anything you feel self-conscious about that you wish you didn't?

_____

_____

_____

IF YOU WERE A _____,
WHAT WOULD YOU BE?

Type of car   Me _____ You _____

Animal   Me _____ You _____

Element (earth, air, fire, water)   Me _____ You _____

Color   Me _____ You _____

Time of day   Me _____ You _____

Item of clothing   Me _____ You _____

Shape   Me _____ You _____

Metal   Me _____ You _____

Shoe   Me _____ You _____

Superhero   Me _____ You _____

Season   Me _____ You _____

Flavor of ice cream   Me _____ You _____

WHAT'S YOUR
SOCIAL STYLE?

Big parties or more intimate gatherings? **Me** _____ **You** _____

A few best friends or many friends and
acquaintances? **Me** _____ **You** _____

Hosting parties at your place or going
to other people's houses? **Me** _____ **You** _____

A new restaurant every night or one place
where everyone knows you? **Me** _____ **You** _____

Making plans with friends individually
or hanging out all together? **Me** _____ **You** _____

Bonding over good conversation
or dancing until 4 A.M.? **Me** _____ **You** _____

Dancing sober or dancing after
a couple drinks? **Me** _____ **You** _____

Karaoke spectator or karaoke singer? **Me** _____ **You** _____

Chatting with someone one-on-one or
talking in a big group? **Me** _____ **You** _____

Doing something active with friends
(softball, yoga) or enjoying a meal
together? **Me** _____ **You** _____

HOW DO YOU LIKE
THE BED?

1. How many pillows do you like when you're sleeping?

2. What kinds of sheets are your favorite?

3. How often do you think sheets should be changed?

4. Covers on or covers off?

5. Which side of the bed do you like best?

6. On which side of your body do you prefer to sleep?

_____

_____

7. What are your worst sleeping habits?

_____

_____

_____

8. What's your biggest pet peeve about my sleeping habits?

_____

_____

_____

9. What's the cutest thing you've seen me do while asleep?

_____

_____

_____

10. What are you most sensitive to while you sleep? (Sound, lights, etc.)

_____

_____

_____

11. What helps you sleep when you're having trouble?

_____

_____

_____

12. How do you ideally like to wake up?

_____

_____

_____

13. How long do you need in the morning to feel totally awake?

_____

_____

_____

14. Do I do anything that inhibits your sleep? If so, what?

_____

_____

_____

15. Do you like to hit the snooze button (repeatedly)?

_____

_____

_____

OUR BIGGEST RELATIONSHIP ANNOYANCES

Constantly asking where stuff is around the house   Me ❑   You ❑

Not being able to make decisions about little things   Me ❑   You ❑

Saying nothing's wrong when something totally is   Me ❑   You ❑

Moving my things around without asking   Me ❑   You ❑

Nagging   Me ❑   You ❑

Being passive-aggressive   Me ❑   You ❑

Harmless flirting with other people   Me ❑   You ❑

Not asking before inviting people over   Me ❑   You ❑

Flaking on plans at the last minute   Me ❑   You ❑

Not having a life outside of the relationship   Me ❑   You ❑

Making plans I'm involved in without asking me   Me ❑   You ❑

Expecting me to pay for everything   Me ❑   You ❑

Letting me do all the cleaning and housework   Me ❑   You ❑

Too much checking up/checking in   Me ❑   You ❑

Not getting enough alone time   Me ❑   You ❑

Not showing enough affection in public   Me ❑   You ❑

Showing too much affection in public   Me ❑   You ❑

You ☐ Me
You ☐ Me
You ☐ Me
You ☐ Me
You ☐ Me
You ☐ Me
You ☐ Me

PLACES TO VISIT, SKIP, OR LIVE
(AROUND THE WORLD)

1. Thailand — **Visit / Skip / Live**

2. New Zealand — **Visit / Skip / Live**

3. Italy — **Visit / Skip / Live**

4. Iceland — **Visit / Skip / Live**

5. Brazil — **Visit / Skip / Live**

6. China — **Visit / Skip / Live**

7. Canada — **Visit / Skip / Live**

8. Fiji — **Visit / Skip / Live**

9. South Africa — **Visit / Skip / Live**

10. Dubai — **Visit / Skip / Live**

11. Japan — **Visit / Skip / Live**

12. Argentina — **Visit / Skip / Live**

13. Egypt — **Visit / Skip / Live**

14. France — **Visit / Skip / Live**

15. Costa Rica — **Visit / Skip / Live**

WHAT YOU WOULD DO IF YOU COULD QUIT YOUR JOB AND STICK IT TO "THE MAN"?

Open a winery   **Me** ❑ | **You** ❑

Open a bed and breakfast   **Me** ❑ | **You** ❑

Sail around the world   **Me** ❑ | **You** ❑

Backpack around Europe   **Me** ❑ | **You** ❑

Move to the mountains   **Me** ❑ | **You** ❑

Live on a deserted island   **Me** ❑ | **You** ❑

Open a bar   **Me** ❑ | **You** ❑

Open your own craft store   **Me** ❑ | **You** ❑

Become a ski/tennis/yoga instructor   **Me** ❑ | **You** ❑

Become a park ranger   **Me** ❑ | **You** ❑

Go back to school   **Me** ❑ | **You** ❑

Volunteer full-time   **Me** ❑ | **You** ❑

Run for public office   **Me** ❑ | **You** ❑

WHAT COULD YOU
LIVE WITHOUT?

... FOR A WEEK:

Coffee or sex?

Me _____ You _____

Driving your car or use of your
smartphone?

Me _____ You _____

Alcohol or fast food?

Me _____ You _____

Dining out or eating dessert?

Me _____ You _____

... FOR A MONTH:

Coffee or sex?

Me _____ You _____

Driving your car or use of your
smartphone?

Me _____ You _____

Alcohol or fast food?

Me _____ You _____

Dining out or eating dessert?

Me _____ You _____

...FOR A YEAR:

Coffee or sex? **Me** _____ **You** _____

Driving your car or use of your
smartphone? **Me** _____ **You** _____

Alcohol or fast food? **Me** _____ **You** _____

Dining out or eating dessert? **Me** _____ **You** _____

...FOREVER:

Coffee or sex? **Me** _____ **You** _____

Driving your car or use of your
smartphone? **Me** _____ **You** _____

Alcohol or fast food? **Me** _____ **You** _____

Dining out or eating dessert? **Me** _____ **You** _____

LET ME HEAR YOUR BODY TALK
(ER . . . OR, LET'S JUST TALK
ABOUT YOUR BODY)

1. Have you ever been overweight, underweight, or struggled with your weight?

_____

_____

_____

2. Do you consider yourself to be a healthy person?

_____

_____

_____

3. Do you have any body or health goals that you haven't told me about?

_____

_____

_____

4. Are you satisfied with your current level of health?

_____

_____

_____

5. How often do you visit the doctor to get checkups?

_____

_____

_____

6. Is there anything bothering you with your body, or anything going on that's out of the ordinary?

_____

_____

_____

7. Have you ever had any kind of disease or medical condition?

_____

_____

_____

8. Do you have a family history of disease?

_____

_____

_____

9. Is there anything I can do to help you be healthier?

_____

_____

_____

10. Do you think there is anything I can do to take better care of myself or be healthier?

_____

_____

_____

LET'S GET AWKWARD AND TALK ABOUT PUBERTY

1. What was the most embarrassing part about going through puberty for you?

_____

_____

_____

2. What was the first thing that changed about your body?

_____

_____

_____

3. What was the last thing that changed?

_____

_____

_____

4. Were you an early developer or a late bloomer?

_____

_____

_____

5. How did you parents deal with puberty and having "the talk"?

_____

_____

_____

6. What's your most cringe-worthy puberty moment?

_____

_____

_____

7. Were you ever caught masturbating as a teenager?

_____

_____

_____

8. Was there any part of puberty of which you were happy or proud about?

_____

_____

_____

9. Did you have acne as a teenager?

_____

_____

_____

10. What was the most surprising thing (at the time) you learned as a teen about sex or your changing body?

_____

_____

_____

THE AFTERLIFE

1. How do you feel about death?

_____

_____

_____

_____

2. What shaped your feelings about death?

_____

_____

_____

_____

3. When did you learn about the concept of death, and from whom?

_____

_____

_____

_____

4. What do you think happens when we die?

_____

_____

_____

_____

5. What shaped your concept of the afterlife (or lack of)?

_____

_____

_____

6. What would your ideal "heaven" be?

_____

_____

_____

_____

7. If reincarnation is real, what would you like to come back as?

_____

_____

_____

_____

8. What worries you the most about death?

_____

_____

_____

_____

9. How many years do you think is ideal to have on the Earth?

_____

_____

_____

_____

10. Is there any reason you can think of why or under what circumstances you might look forward to death?

_____

_____

_____

11. If given the chance, would you drink from the fountain of youth and live forever?

_____

_____

_____

_____

12. If there is an afterlife, who do you hope will greet you on the other side?

_____

_____

_____

_____

"CITY WE LIVE IN" BUCKET LIST

Try every restaurant	Me ❑	You ❑
Visit every museum	Me ❑	You ❑
Pretend to be tourists and check out all the attractions one day	Me ❑	You ❑
Climb the highest local peak	Me ❑	You ❑
Invite our neighbors over for dinner	Me ❑	You ❑
Book a room at the fanciest hotel in town for one night	Me ❑	You ❑
Go camping locally	Me ❑	You ❑
Participate in a local charity event	Me ❑	You ❑
Spend a morning hitting all the local garage sales	Me ❑	You ❑
Walk in a holiday parade	Me ❑	You ❑
Meet our elected officials	Me ❑	You ❑
Volunteer at our neighborhood animal shelter	Me ❑	You ❑
Partake in a pub-crawl	Me ❑	You ❑

HAPPY BIRTHDAY!
(OR NOT . . .)

1. Do you like celebrating your birthday?

_____

_____

_____

2. What's your ideal way to mark the occasion?

_____

_____

_____

3. What was your best birthday?

_____

_____

_____

4. What was your most memorable birthday party as a kid?

_____

_____

_____

5. What's the craziest thing you ever asked for on your birthday?

_____

_____

_____

6. What's your favorite type of birthday cake?

_____

_____

7. How do you feel about surprise parties?

_____

_____

_____

8. Are you down with people singing "Happy Birthday" to you in a restaurant?

_____

_____

_____

9. Do you prefer people to call you, e-mail you, or text you on your birthday?

_____

_____

_____

10. Does your family have any birthday traditions?

_____

_____

_____

You □ Me
You □ Me
You □ Me
You □ Me
You □ Me
You □ Me
You □ Me
You □ Me

WOULD YOU RATHER?

Skydive or bungee jump? ° Become president or become
...ty? ° Buy a huge ...ch or your own a private island? ° In...
something that ch...ges the world or win the lottery? ° Ch...
...le in Be...
...t song? ° Go to ...
...val in Rio or do ...ming with the ...lls in Spain? ° Join

WHICH ROMANTIC SURPRISE WOULD YOU PREFER?

Cute note on the bathroom mirror or
love-letter e-mail? **Me** _____ **You** _____

Flowers or favorite dessert? **Me** _____ **You** _____

Picnic in the park in the daytime or
stargazing in the park at night? **Me** _____ **You** _____

Reservations at a hot new restaurant or
a home-cooked dinner? **Me** _____ **You** _____

A clean bathroom or a clean kitchen? **Me** _____ **You** _____

A bubble bath or a massage? **Me** _____ **You** _____

A naughty voicemail or a steamy sext? **Me** _____ **You** _____

Breakfast in bed or morning sex? **Me** _____ **You** _____

A washed car or a made bed? **Me** _____ **You** _____

A scenic drive or a stroll through
our neighborhood? **Me** _____ **You** _____

FIGHTING WORDS: DEALING WITH CONFLICT IN OUR RELATIONSHIP

1. How does it make you feel when we fight?

_____

_____

_____

2. How much fighting is too much in a relationship?

_____

_____

_____

3. What's the worst thing I do when we fight?

_____

_____

_____

4. What do you think is the worst thing you do?

_____

_____

_____

5. What could I do to help you stop being mad at me when we fight?

_____

_____

_____

6. Would you ever consider going to couple's counseling?

_____

_____

_____

7. How do you think we both manage problems and conflicts?

_____

_____

_____

8. What are some of the unsolvable issues we tend to fight about, and do you think we can ever resolve them?

_____

_____

_____

9. What personality traits of mine do you think cause issues in our relationship?

_____

_____

_____

10. What personality traits of yours do you think cause issues in our relationship?

_____

_____

_____

11. Can some fights be solved with a hug?

_____

_____

You ☐ Me
You ☐ Me
You ☐ Me
You ☐ Me
You ☐ Me
You ☐ Me
You ☐ Me
You ☐ Me

WHAT'S YOUR IDEAL WEDDING?

Elope or have a traditional celebration? **Me** _____ **You** _____

Have a wedding close to home or
a destination wedding? **Me** _____ **You** _____

Large wedding or small wedding? **Me** _____ **You** _____

Indoor or outdoor? **Me** _____ **You** _____

Band or DJ? **Me** _____ **You** _____

Daytime or nighttime? **Me** _____ **You** _____

Bridal party or no attendants? **Me** _____ **You** _____

Religious ceremony or
nondenominational? **Me** _____ **You** _____

Sit-down meal or buffet? **Me** _____ **You** _____

Huge cake or dessert bar? **Me** _____ **You** _____

Rowdy bachelor/bachelorette parties or
low-key guys/girls weekends? **Me** _____ **You** _____

Heartfelt or funny/embarrassing
speeches? **Me** _____ **You** _____

Traditional or writing your own vows? **Me** _____ **You** _____

THE BEST OF US

1. What's your favorite memory with me?

_____

_____

_____

2. What's your favorite trip we've taken?

_____

_____

_____

3. What's your favorite date we've been on?

_____

_____

_____

4. What's the best thing you've learned about love from our relationship?

_____

_____

_____

5. What's the best thing I've taught you since we've been together?

_____

_____

_____

6. What's the best change you've seen in yourself since we've been together?

_____

_____

_____

7. What the best change you've seen in me since we've started dating?

_____

_____

_____

8. What's the best sexual experience we've had together?

_____

_____

_____

9. What's the all-around best part about our relationship?

_____

_____

_____

10. What quality in our relationship would you feel sad to lose?

_____

_____

_____

11. What's your favorite photo of us?

_____

_____

_____

You ☐ Me ☰
ou ☐ Me ☲
ou ☐ ☐ ☐
ou ☐ Me ☷
ou ☐ ☐ ☐
ou ☐ Me ☶
ou ☐ ☐ ☐

YOU CAN TELL ME ANYTHING, RIGHT? UNDER WHAT CIRCUMSTANCES WOULD YOU . . .

1. Do pornography?

_____

_____

_____

2. Rob a bank?

_____

_____

_____

3. Murder someone?

_____

_____

_____

4. Consider suicide?

_____

_____

_____

5. Steal from a relative?

_____

_____

_____

WOULD YOU RATHER?

Skydive or bungee jump? * Become president or become
buy a huge ranch or your own a private island? * In
something that changes the world or win the lottery? * C
Mount Everest or scuba-dive the Great Blue Hole in Be
* Publish a bestselling book or write a hit song? * Go to
nival in Rio or do running with the bulls in Spain? * Join

6. Have sex for money?

7. Sell drugs?

8. Commit cannibalism?

9. Commit fraud?

10. Steal from your company?

HOW ANNOYING ARE THESE COMMON PET PEEVES? (PART 2)

1. People who don't pick up after their dogs
   A lot / A little / Not at all

2. People who take up two parking spaces
   A lot / A little / Not at all

3. People who come into work when they're sick
   A lot / A little / Not at all

4. People who leave big clumps of their hair in the shower drain
   A lot / A little / Not at all

5. People who take up both armrests on airplanes
   A lot / A little / Not at all

6. People who put their feet on the seat in front of them in movie theaters
   A lot / A little / Not at all

7. People who insist on just splitting the bill at a group dinner, when you all had different quantities of food and drink
   A lot / A little / Not at all

8. People who have private cell phone conversations in public places
   A lot / A little / Not at all

9. People who are indecisive about little things, like where to go for dinner
   A lot / A little / Not at all

10. People who don't hold doors open for others
    A lot / A little / Not at all

WOULD YOU RATHER?

Skydive or bungee jump? Become president or become...
...Buy a huge... or your own a private island?...
something that changes the world or win the lottery?...
...Blue Hole... Beli...
Publish a bestselling book or write a hit song? Go to C...
...nival in Rio or do running with the bulls in Spain? Join...

OUR PERSONALITIES

1. What's your favorite quality of mine?

_____

_____

2. What's your favorite quality of yours?

_____

_____

3. What's something I do well that I don't do enough?

_____

_____

4. What's my most annoying quality?

_____

_____

5. If you could change something about me, what would it be?

_____

_____

6. If I could pass down one quality of mine to our kids, what would you hope it would be?

_____

_____

7. What are my destructive personality traits?

_____

_____

8. What's your most destructive personality trait?

_____

9. What do you think my best talent is?

_____

_____

10. In one word, how would you describe me?

_____

_____

11. In one word, how would you describe yourself?

_____

_____

12. What do you think other people admire about me?

_____

_____

13. What do you hope other people admire about you?

_____

_____

14. How do you think my personality complements yours?

_____

_____

15. What part of your personality was superstrong, even when you were a child?

_____

_____

WOULD YOU RATHER?

Skydive or bungee jump? * Become president or become r
...y? * Buy a huge ...ch or your own a private island? * ...
something that cha...ges the world or win the lottery? * Cl...
...Hole in Beli...
* Publish a bestselling book or write a hit song? * Go to C...
...rval in Rio or do running with the bulls in Spain? * Join...

BODY SCAVENGER HUNT

1. Do you have attached earlobes or detached earlobes?

   Me _____ **You** _____

2. Do you have webbed toes or nonwebbed toes?

   Me _____ **You** _____

3. Do you have a widow's peak or straight hairline?

   Me _____ **You** _____

4. Is your second toe longer or shorter than your big toe?

   Me _____ **You** _____

5. Do you clasp your hands with your right thumb over your left or left over right?

   Me _____ **You** _____

6. Which leg is in front when you cross your legs Indian style?

   Me _____ **You** _____

7. Is your thumb angled or straight when you give a "thumbs up" sign?

   Me _____ **You** _____

8. Do you have a small bump on the inside of your upper ear or is it smooth?

   Me _____ **You** _____

9. Does your pinkie bend straight down or to the side?

   Me _____ **You** _____

10. Does your hair curl clockwise or counterclockwise at the back of your head?

    Me _____ **You** _____

HOW DO YOU FEEL
ABOUT THESE COMMON
RELATIONSHIP TRUISMS?

1. Relationships take a lot of work.
   Agree because . . . Disagree because . . . It's not so cut-and-dried because . . .

   _____

   _____

   _____

   _____

2. Absence makes the heart grow fonder.
   Agree because . . . Disagree because . . . It's not so cut-and-dried because . . .

   _____

   _____

   _____

   _____

3. Nice guys finish last.
   Agree because . . . Disagree because . . . It's not so cut-and-dried because . . .

   _____

   _____

   _____

   _____

4. Men and women can't just be friends.
   Agree because ... Disagree because ... It's not so cut-and-dried because ...

   _____

   _____

   _____

5. Love is a decision.
   Agree because ... Disagree because ... It's not so cut-and-dried because ...

   _____

   _____

   _____

   _____

6. You are responsible for your own emotions.
   Agree because ... Disagree because ... It's not so cut-and-dried because ...

   _____

   _____

   _____

   _____

7. Without communication, even the strongest relationships can fall apart.
   Agree because ... Disagree because ... It's not so cut-and-dried because ...

   _____

   _____

   _____

   _____

8. You should put your marriage (or relationship) first.
   Agree because ... Disagree because ... It's not so cut-and-dried because ...

   _____
   _____
   _____

9. Once a cheater, always a cheater.
   Agree because ... Disagree because ... It's not so cut-and-dried because ...

   _____
   _____
   _____
   _____

10. Women are more emotional than men.
    Agree because ... Disagree because ... It's not so cut-and-dried because ...

    _____
    _____
    _____
    _____

11. Love means never having to say you're sorry.
    Agree because ... Disagree because ... It's not so cut-and-dried because ...

    _____
    _____
    _____
    _____

I THINK WE'RE ALONE NOW ...
OR AT LEAST I KINDA
WISH WE WERE

1. What would you do with your free time if you were single?

_____

_____

_____

2. What's a healthy amount of time for us to spend apart?

_____

_____

_____

3. How would you feel if I took a vacation by myself?

_____

_____

_____

4. How would you feel if I took a vacation with friends but without you?

_____

_____

_____

5. How many nights per week should we spend with friends, coworkers, or just other people?

_____

_____

_____

6. Do you feel like you get enough time by yourself?

_____

_____

7. What do you like to do when you spend time alone?

_____

_____

_____

8. What do you think the value is in both of us spending some time apart?

_____

_____

_____

9. What do you think happens when couples spend too much time together?

_____

_____

_____

10. How often should we spend time together without our kids?

_____

_____

_____

11. How much one-on-one time should each of us have with our kids?

_____

_____

HOW WOULD YOU REACT TO THESE SCENARIOS?

1. How would you feel if you had a gay child?
   **Wouldn't bother me because ... Would bother me because ...
   I have mixed feelings because ...**

   _____

   _____

   _____

   _____

   _____

2. How do you feel about the woman being the breadwinner in the family?
   **Wouldn't bother me because ... Would bother me because ...
   I have mixed feelings because ...**

   _____

   _____

   _____

   _____

3. How would you feel if your child married someone outside of our religion?
   **Wouldn't bother me because ... Would bother me because ...
   I have mixed feelings because ...**

   _____

   _____

   _____

4. How would you feel if your child married someone outside of our race?
Wouldn't bother me because ... Would bother me because ...
I have mixed feelings because ...

_____

_____

_____

_____

_____

_____

5. How would you feel if I wanted to buy a gun?
Wouldn't bother me because ... Would bother me because ...
I have mixed feelings because ...

_____

_____

_____

_____

_____

6. How would you feel about spanking a child?
Wouldn't bother me because ... Would bother me because ...
I have mixed feelings because ...

_____

_____

_____

7. How would you feel about adopting a child?
   **Wouldn't bother me because . . . Would bother me because . . .
   I have mixed feelings because . . .**

   _____

   _____

   _____

   _____

   _____

   _____

8. How would you feel if we got pregnant and considered getting an abortion?
   **Wouldn't bother me because . . . Would bother me because . . .
   I have mixed feelings because . . .**

   _____

   _____

   _____

   _____

   _____

9. Would you be willing to pull the plug on me if I became a vegetable?
   **Wouldn't bother me because . . . Would bother me because . . .
   I have mixed feelings because . . .**

   _____

   _____

   _____

   _____

10. How would you feel if I wanted to get a sex change?

Wouldn't bother me because ... Would bother me because ...
I have mixed feelings because ...

_____

_____

_____

_____

_____

_____

WOULD YOU RATHER?
Skydive or bungee jump? * Become president or become
ality? * Buy a huge ... ch or your own a private island? * In
something that changes the world or win the lottery? * Cl
... * Publish a bestselling book or write a hit song? * Go to C
... nival in Rio or do running with the bulls in Spain? * Join

OUR SEXUAL FANTASIES

Getting tied up	Me ❑	You ❑
Tying someone up	Me ❑	You ❑
Role-playing: Schoolgirl/professor	Me ❑	You ❑
Domination	Me ❑	You ❑
Voyeurism	Me ❑	You ❑
Role-playing: Rock star/groupie	Me ❑	You ❑
Anal play	Me ❑	You ❑
Sex in a public place	Me ❑	You ❑
Striptease	Me ❑	You ❑
Role-playing: Pretending we're strangers	Me ❑	You ❑
Swinging	Me ❑	You ❑
Role-playing: Naughty nurse/patient	Me ❑	You ❑
Using blindfolds	Me ❑	You ❑
Watching porn together	Me ❑	You ❑
Making porn together	Me ❑	You ❑
Using a vibrator together	Me ❑	You ❑

WOULD YOU RATHER?

Skydive or bungee jump? * Become president or become
ally? * Buy a huge ranch or your own a private island? * In
something that changes the world or win the lottery? * C
... Blue Hole in Be
* Publish a bestselling book or write a hit song? * Go to
nival in Rio or do running with the bulls in Spain? * Join

HOW DO WE LOOK?

1. What's your favorite body part of mine?

_____

_____

_____

2. What's your favorite part on your own body?

_____

_____

_____

3. When do you think I am most attractive?

_____

_____

_____

4. What did you find most attractive about me when we first met?

_____

_____

_____

5. What's your favorite haircut I've had since we've known each other?

_____

_____

_____

6. If you were my stylist, how would you change my appearance or clothing choices?

_____

_____

_____

7. What's your favorite outfit that I wear?

_____

_____

_____

8. What piece of clothing or outfit makes you feel your physical best?

_____

_____

_____

9. How do you think my looks have changed since we met?

_____

_____

_____

10. In what way would you never want me to drastically change my appearance?

_____

_____

_____

11. What physical quality do you hope we each pass on to our kids?

_____

_____

_____

12. Would you ever consider getting plastic surgery?

13. What are you most dreading about the physical aging process?

14. Will you dye your hair when you go gray?

15. If you were losing your hair, would you take medication to stop or slow the process?

16. Who do you think you look most like (from your family, a celebrity, etc.)?

You ☐ Me
You ☐ Me
You ☐ Me
You ☐ Me
You ☐ Me
You ☐ Me
You ☐ Me
You ☐ Me

WOULD YOU RATHER?
Skydive or bungee jump? * Become president or become
alty? * Buy a huge ranch or your own a private island? * Inv
something that changes the world or win the lottery? * Cl
Hole in Bel
Go to G
in Spain? * Join

ACTIVITIES YOU LOVED
AS A KID (AND MAY STILL LOVE
NOW—NO JUDGMENT!)

Foosball or ping pong?   Me _____   You _____

Magic: The Gathering or Pokémon?   Me _____   You _____

Flag football or tackle football?   Me _____   You _____

Capture the Flag or Ultimate Frisbee?   Me _____   You _____

Sega or Nintendo?   Me _____   You _____

Duck Hunt or *Paperboy*?   Me _____   You _____

Playing MASH or playing with a
Ouija board?   Me _____   You _____

Water balloon fight or Super Soaker?   Me _____   You _____

Roller-skating or ice-skating?   Me _____   You _____

Waterskiing or snow skiing?   Me _____   You _____

Skee ball or pinball?   Me _____   You _____

Ballet or jazz?   Me _____   You _____

Soccer or baseball?   Me _____   You _____

Red Rover or Tug of War?   Me _____   You _____

Spying on neighbors or TP'ing houses?   Me _____   You _____

You □ Me
You □ Me
You □ Me
You □ Me
You □ Me
You □ Me
You □ Me
You □ Me

WOULD YOU RATHER?
Skydive or bungee jump? * Become president or become
ity? * Buy a huge yacht or your own a private island? * In
something that changes the world or win the lottery? * O
Hole in Be
a hit song? * Go to
nival in Rio or do running with the bulls in Spain? * Jair

LET'S REVEAL HOW WEIRD
OUR BODIES ARE

1. What do you think is your funniest-looking body part?

_____

_____

_____

2. Where's the weirdest place you have a freckle?

_____

_____

_____

3. Where's the weirdest place you have hair?

_____

_____

_____

4. What's the most embarrassing beauty or body product you use?

_____

_____

_____

5. Do you wax or shave anything I don't know about?

_____

_____

_____

6. What's your coolest scar, and how did you get it?

_____

_____

_____

7. Do you have any allergies?

_____

_____

_____

8. What's the craziest thing that's ever happened to your body (like a weird physical reaction)?

_____

_____

_____

9. Are there any places you hate being touched?

_____

_____

_____

10. Where are you most ticklish?

_____

_____

_____

OUR DREAM HOUSE

Big backyard	Me ❑	You ❑
Great view	Me ❑	You ❑
Eat-in kitchen	Me ❑	You ❑
Open concept	Me ❑	You ❑
Master bedroom	Me ❑	You ❑
Soaker tub in the master bathroom	Me ❑	You ❑
Spare bedrooms	Me ❑	You ❑
Window seat for reading	Me ❑	You ❑
High-end kitchen appliances	Me ❑	You ❑
Porch or balcony	Me ❑	You ❑
Pool or hot tub	Me ❑	You ❑
Vegetable garden	Me ❑	You ❑
Entertaining space	Me ❑	You ❑
Media room	Me ❑	You ❑
Hardwood floors	Me ❑	You ❑

Family-friendly neighborhood	Me ❑	You ❑
Close to restaurants and nightlife	Me ❑	You ❑
Close to family	Me ❑	You ❑
Far from city center	Me ❑	You ❑
Penthouse apartment	Me ❑	You ❑
Wet bar	Me ❑	You ❑
Man (or woman) cave	Me ❑	You ❑

WHO COMES OUT ON TOP IN THESE HYPOTHETICAL SITUATIONS?

1. Win a spontaneous karaoke contest?   Me ❏ ‖ You ❏

2. Get hit on the most at a singles event?   Me ❏ ‖ You ❏

3. Dominate in Trivial Pursuit?   Me ❏ ‖ You ❏

4. Make it to the top of the hike first?   Me ❏ ‖ You ❏

5. Bring down the house at a comedy club's open mic night?   Me ❏ ‖ You ❏

6. Get a better score on cartwheel technique in a gymnastics competition?   Me ❏ ‖ You ❏

7. Create an artistic masterpiece?   Me ❏ ‖ You ❏

8. Become a professional eater?   Me ❏ ‖ You ❏

9. Win a drinking contest?   Me ❏ ‖ You ❏

10. Win a tightrope competition?   Me ❏ ‖ You ❏

11. Solve the *New York Times* Sunday crossword first?   Me ❏ ‖ You ❏

12. Become a Broadway star?   Me ❏ ‖ You ❏

13. Win an amateur stripping contest?   Me ❏ ‖ You ❏

WHAT'S YOUR WORLDVIEW?

1. How informed do you like to be about world events?

_____

_____

2. Do you think it's more important to help out people in our country first before helping those in other countries?

_____

_____

3. If you had to pick one foreign country in which to live for the rest of your life, which would it be?

_____

_____

4. Are there certain places in the world to which you know you would never want to go?

_____

_____

5. If you were to learn another language, what would it be?

_____

_____

6. What global issue do you care about the most?

_____

_____

7. Which countries or people do you feel are most in need right now?

_____

_____

8. Do you worry about the threat of war?

_____

_____

_____

9. Do you worry about climate change?

_____

_____

_____

10. Is there a place in the world or a world issue you wish you knew more about?

_____

_____

_____

11. Do you think the world is a safe place, collectively?

_____

_____

_____

12. How comfortable are you traveling to places where you don't know the language or culture?

_____

_____

_____

PLACES TO VISIT,
SKIP, OR LIVE
(AROUND THE UNITED STATES)

1. Los Angeles — **Visit / Skip / Live**

2. Small town, U.S.A. — **Visit / Skip / Live**

3. New York City — **Visit / Skip / Live**

4. Chicago — **Visit / Skip / Live**

5. Miami — **Visit / Skip / Live**

6. San Francisco — **Visit / Skip / Live**

7. Las Vegas — **Visit / Skip / Live**

8. Austin — **Visit / Skip / Live**

9. Washington, D.C. — **Visit / Skip / Live**

10. Boston — **Visit / Skip / Live**

11. Nashville — **Visit / Skip / Live**

12. St. Louis — **Visit / Skip / Live**

13. Jackson Hole — **Visit / Skip / Live**

14. Atlanta — **Visit / Skip / Live**

You ☐ Me
You ☐ Me
You ☐ Me
You ☐ Me
You ☐ Me
You ☐ Me
You ☐ Me

WOULD YOU RATHER?

Skydive or bungee jump? * Become president or become
alty? * Buy a huge ranch or your own a private island? * In
something that changes the world or win the lottery? * C
Me... ...reat Blue Hole in the
* Publish a bestselling book or write a hit song? * Go to
nival in Rio or do running with the bulls in Spain? * Jo

OUR FIRST DATE

1. If you had to describe our first date with a song, which one would you choose?

_____

_____

_____

2. What do you remember most about our first date?

_____

_____

_____

3. Did you have any reservations about going on the date or were you nervous about it?

_____

_____

_____

4. What did you like about me then that you still like now?

_____

_____

_____

5. Why did you ask me out/agree to go out with me in the first place?

_____

_____

_____

WOULD YOU RATHER?

Skydive or bungee jump? Become president or become r...
your own a private island? Inv...
something that changes the world or win the lottery? Cli...
Mount Everest or scuba-dive the Great Blue Hole in Beli...
Publish a bestselling book or write a hit song? Go to C...
nival in Rio or do running with the bulls in Spain? Join...

6. What were your expectations for the date?

_____

_____

_____

7. Did you see any red flags early on, and if so, what were they?

_____

_____

_____

8. Is there anything you'd change about our first date?

_____

_____

_____

9. What would you tell our kids about our first date?

_____

_____

_____

10. Who did you talk to after our first date about how it went? (And what did you say?)

_____

_____

_____

WOULD YOU RATHER?
Skydive or bungee jump? * Become president or become re...
...ry? * Buy a huge ...ch or your own a private island? * love...
...something that ch...ges the world or win the lottery? * Clim...
...Hole to Beliz...
...Go to Ca...
...ival in Rio or do running with the bulls in Spain? * Join t...

DEALING WITH CH-CH-CH-CHANGES IN RELATIONSHIPS

1. How do you think you've changed since we started dating?

_____

_____

_____

2. How have I changed since we started dating?

_____

_____

_____

3. Is there anything I used to do that you wish I still did?

_____

_____

_____

4. Anything you used to do when we started dating that you regret losing?

_____

_____

_____

5. How do you think our relationship has evolved?

_____

_____

_____

6. What's one thing you hope never changes in our relationship?

_____

_____

7. What's one thing you want to change about our relationship?

_____

_____

_____

8. Do you think it's possible for people to really change?

_____

_____

_____

9. If I needed you to change a habit or behavior, would you be willing to do so?

_____

_____

_____

10. Do you think it's acceptable to break up with someone if he or she drastically changes over time?

_____

_____

_____

WHO WOULD YOU TRUST IN THESE HYPOTHETICAL EMERGENCY SITUATIONS?

1. Give a stranger mouth-to-mouth — Me ❏ | You ❏

2. Pull out a bee stinger if one of us got stung — Me ❏ | You ❏

3. Be able to talk his or her way out of a speeding ticket — Me ❏ | You ❏

4. Fly a plane in a crisis — Me ❏ | You ❏

5. Survive in a boat in the middle of the ocean — Me ❏ | You ❏

6. Survive on a deserted island — Me ❏ | You ❏

7. Survive a zombie apocalypse — Me ❏ | You ❏

8. Drive the getaway car — Me ❏ | You ❏

9. Rob a bank — Me ❏ | You ❏

10. Lie on command to avoid getting in trouble — Me ❏ | You ❏

11. Fly a jet into the heart of an alien spaceship, effectively saving the world — Me ❏ | You ❏

12. Fight off a bear — Me ❏ | You ❏

TALKING ABOUT YOUR J-O-B
(OR, QUESTIONS YOU ANSWER
IN AN INTERVIEW)

1. What is a typical day at work like for you?

_____

_____

_____

2. What's the most rewarding part of your job?

_____

_____

_____

3. What's the least rewarding or most frustrating part of your job?

_____

_____

_____

4. What made you go into your field?

_____

_____

_____

5. What do you ultimately envision yourself doing, career-wise?

_____

_____

_____

6. How important is it to you that people respect your career path?

_____

_____

_____

7. How do you define success?

_____

_____

_____

8. What other jobs or career tracks could you see yourself pursuing in the future?

_____

_____

_____

9. What would it take for you to quit a job?

_____

_____

_____

10. What would it take for you to leave a job that paid well, but that you didn't like?

_____

_____

_____

WOULD YOU RATHER?

Skydive or bungee jump? Become president or become
aly? Buy a huge yacht or your own a private island? In
something that changes the world or win the lottery? Cl
Blue Hole in Bel
hit song? Go to C
val in Rio or do running with the bulls in Spain? Join

DO YOU HAVE ANY HIDDEN TALENTS?

Juggling **Me** ☐ **You** ☐

Unicycling **Me** ☐ **You** ☐

Six-minute-mile running **Me** ☐ **You** ☐

High-jumping **Me** ☐ **You** ☐

Typing crazy-fast **Me** ☐ **You** ☐

Video gaming **Me** ☐ **You** ☐

Crossword puzzle completing **Me** ☐ **You** ☐

Fire-eating **Me** ☐ **You** ☐

Magic trick performing **Me** ☐ **You** ☐

Tap-dancing **Me** ☐ **You** ☐

Burping on command **Me** ☐ **You** ☐

Burping the alphabet **Me** ☐ **You** ☐

Puppeteering **Me** ☐ **You** ☐

Horse (or pet) whispering **Me** ☐ **You** ☐

LET'S GET PHYSICAL...
BUT NOT IN THAT WAY

1. Do you consider yourself an active person?

_____

_____

_____

2. Are you more active now or when you were younger?

_____

_____

_____

3. Do you wish you were more active than you are?

_____

_____

_____

4. What are your fitness goals?

_____

_____

_____

5. Do you think we need to be more active?

_____

_____

_____

6. How would you feel if you suddenly gained a lot of weight?

_____

_____

7. How would you feel if I did?

_____

_____

_____

8. If you were to gain a lot of weight, how would you go about losing it?

_____

_____

_____

9. If I did, how would you encourage me to lose it?

_____

_____

_____

10. If you were stuck in a fitness rut, what do you think about trying out a yoga class, joining an adult sports league, or something active outside of your comfort zone?

_____

_____

_____

11. What's your favorite way to exercise?

_____

_____

_____

WHAT WOULD YOU NAME YOUR KID IF YOU WANTED HIM/HER TO BECOME A . . .

1. Quarterback?

_____

_____

2. Computer scientist?

_____

_____

3. CEO?

_____

_____

4. Rock star?

_____

_____

5. Doctor?

_____

_____

6. Tennis star?

_____

_____

7. Llama herder?

_____

_____

8. Fashion designer?

_____

_____

9. Olympic skier?

_____

_____

10. President?

_____

_____

11. Member of the Peace Corps?

_____

_____

12. Mob boss?

_____

_____

COMMON CHARACTERISTICS (PART 2)

1. Who is more easily embarrassed?   **Me** ❏ | **You** ❏

2. Who is more curious?   **Me** ❏ | **You** ❏

3. Who is more gullible?   **Me** ❏ | **You** ❏

4. Who is more easily discouraged?   **Me** ❏ | **You** ❏

5. Who is more shy?   **Me** ❏ | **You** ❏

6. Who is more cautious?   **Me** ❏ | **You** ❏

7. Who is more paranoid?   **Me** ❏ | **You** ❏

8. Who is more indecisive?   **Me** ❏ | **You** ❏

9. Who is more easily excitable?   **Me** ❏ | **You** ❏

10. Who is more mischievous?   **Me** ❏ | **You** ❏

11. Who takes longer to get ready?   **Me** ❏ | **You** ❏

SEXUAL
BUCKET LIST

Sex in public	Me ❑	You ❑
Sex on a beach	Me ❑	You ❑
Sex in the car	Me ❑	You ❑
Tantric sex	Me ❑	You ❑
Group sex or threesome	Me ❑	You ❑
Sex on an airplane	Me ❑	You ❑
Go through the entire Kama Sutra	Me ❑	You ❑
Sex on a boat	Me ❑	You ❑
Phone sex	Me ❑	You ❑
Sex while in an "altered" state	Me ❑	You ❑
Sex in a tent	Me ❑	You ❑
Watch other people have sex live	Me ❑	You ❑

OUR POLITICAL BELIEFS

1. How political would you say you are?

_____

_____

_____

2. When did you start developing your political beliefs?

_____

_____

_____

3. Who do you think has been most influential in terms of your political beliefs?

_____

_____

_____

4. Do you believe that it's important for people to vote, and if so, why?

_____

_____

_____

5. What do you think is the most pressing political issue right now?

_____

_____

_____

6. What issue do you think gets too much attention?

_____

_____

_____

7. What frustrates you most about politics in this country?

_____

_____

_____

8. Who do you think was our best president?

_____

_____

_____

9. How do you feel about women being elected to positions of power and authority?

_____

_____

_____

10. Would you ever consider running for political office?

_____

_____

_____

You ☐ Me
You ☐ Me
You ☐ Me
You ☐ Me
You ☐ Me
You ☐ Me
You ☐ Me

WOULD YOU RATHER?

Skydive or bungee jump? * Become president or become ...
... ? * Buy a huge ... or your own a private island? * In...
something that changes the world or win the lottery? * Cl...
... * ... Blue Hole in Bel...
* Publish a ... or write a hit song? * Go to C...
... in Rio or do running with the bulls in Spain? * Join...

HOW ADVENTUROUS
ARE YOU?

1. What's the weirdest food you've tried?

_____

_____

_____

2. Would you ever consider jumping out of a plane?

_____

_____

_____

3. Would you ever do something that was illegal just for the thrill?

_____

_____

_____

4. Who's the most interesting person you've met while traveling?

_____

_____

_____

5. What's the craziest stunt you've ever done, either as a kid or an adult?

_____

_____

_____

6. What's one "daring" thing you would never do?

_____

7. What's the most daring thing you've ever done?

_____

_____

_____

8. Do you think I'm an adventurous person?

_____

_____

_____

9. Do you wish you were more adventurous? (If yes, in what way?)

_____

_____

_____

10. What's the biggest adventure on your bucket list?

_____

_____

_____

LAW OF ATTRACTION

1. What qualities are you attracted to emotionally?

_____

_____

_____

2. What qualities are you attracted to sexually?

_____

_____

_____

3. Which of these do I possess?

_____

_____

_____

4. What's your biggest turn-on?

_____

_____

_____

5. What's your biggest turnoff?

_____

_____

_____

6. If you watch porn, what kinds of scenarios do you typically seek out?

_____

_____

_____

7. How important do you think physical attraction is in a relationship?

_____

_____

_____

8. If you stopped being sexually attracted to me, how would you handle the situation?

_____

_____

_____

9. What can I do to be more sexually attractive to you?

_____

_____

_____

10. What do you do to make sure I stay interested in and attracted to you?

_____

_____

_____

WOULD YOU RATHER?

Skydive or bungee jump? * Become president or become r
alty? * Buy a huge ranch or your own a private island? * Inv
something that changes the world or win the lottery? * Cli
Publish a bestselling book or write a hit song? * Go to C
nval in Rio or do running with the bulls in Spain? * Join

YOUR PARENTS' RELATIONSHIP

1. In one word, how would you describe your parents' relationship?

_____

_____

_____

2. What's the biggest lesson about partnership or marriage you've learned from them?

_____

_____

_____

3. What about your parents' relationship would you want to replicate in ours?

_____

_____

_____

4. How do you want our relationship to be different than your parents'?

_____

_____

_____

5. How do you think your relationship style has been influenced by your parents?

_____

_____

_____

6. How did your parents handle conflict in front of you when you were younger?

_____

_____

_____

7. How affectionate were your parents in front of you when you were growing up?

_____

_____

_____

8. How has your parents' marriage affected how you feel about divorce?

_____

_____

_____

9. Is there anything about me that reminds you of your mom or dad?

_____

_____

_____

10. Who was in control in your parents' relationship, or was it pretty equal?

_____

_____

_____

WHAT'S YOUR
SOCIAL MEDIA STYLE?

1. How do you feel about the rise of social media in general?

_____

_____

_____

2. Do you prefer Facebook or Twitter?

_____

_____

_____

3. Are you more into blogging or reading other people's blogs?

_____

_____

_____

4. How do you feel about posting photos on Facebook?

_____

_____

_____

5. How do you feel about other people posting photos of you or tagging you in photos?

_____

_____

_____

6. Do you prefer to be active on social media or passive?

_____

_____

_____

7. How do you feel about putting your relationship status on Facebook?

_____

_____

_____

8. Are you more inclined to update your Facebook status weekly, daily, or monthly?

_____

_____

_____

9. How often do you check your social media accounts?

_____

_____

_____

10. Do you prefer people commenting on your social media activity, or "liking" it?

_____

_____

_____

11. Do you prefer to "like" other people's activity, or comment on it?

_____

_____

_____

12. In what ways do you think social media positively influences our lives?

_____

_____

_____

13. In what ways do you think it negatively impacts our lives?

_____

_____

_____

14. What's your biggest social media pet peeve?

_____

_____

_____

15. Have you considered totally unplugging from social media?

_____

_____

_____

WOULD YOU RATHER?

Skydive or bungee jump? * Become president or become r
alty? * Buy a huge yacht or your own a private island? * Inv
something that changes the world or win the lottery? * Cli
Mount Everest or dive the Great Blue Hole in Beli
favorite song? * Go to Co
nival in Rio or do running with the bulls in Spain? * Join

WHAT'S YOUR
FUNNIEST MEMORY?

1. From elementary school?

_____

_____

_____

2. With your parents?

_____

_____

_____

3. From a family vacation?

_____

_____

_____

4. With your best friend?

_____

_____

_____

5. From college?

_____

_____

_____

6. From a story your parents told you about their childhoods?

_____

_____

_____

7. With one of your grandparents?

_____

_____

_____

8. With your siblings?

_____

_____

_____

9. About one of your pets?

_____

_____

_____

10. From camp or playing sports as a kid?

_____

_____

_____

FRIENDSHIPS LOST

1. What's the biggest falling-out you've ever had with a friend?

_____

_____

_____

2. What's your relationship with this person like now?

_____

_____

_____

3. How would you feel if you bumped into this person randomly?

_____

_____

_____

4. Is there someone from your past you wish you still kept in touch with?

_____

_____

_____

5. What's the worst thing a friend has ever done to you?

_____

_____

_____

WOULD YOU RATHER?

Skydive or bungee jump? * Become president or become
something that changes the world or win the lottery? * C
Mount Everest or scuba-dive the Great Blue Hole in Bel
* Publish a bestselling book or write a hit song? * Go to C
nival in Rio or do running with the bulls in Spain? * Join

6. Do you have any true enemies?

_____

_____

7. Have you ever had to "break up" with a friend, and completely sever the relationship?

_____

_____

_____

8. Have you ever betrayed a friend's trust?

_____

_____

_____

9. What's the biggest regret you have in terms of your friendships?

_____

_____

_____

10. Which friend from your past do you think had the worst influence on you?

_____

_____

_____

HOW DO YOU FEEL ABOUT THESE COMMON RELATIONSHIP "RULES"?

1. Don't go to bed mad.

Agree because ... Disagree because ... A little bit of both because ...

_____

_____

_____

_____

_____

2. Never marry someone your family doesn't approve of.

Agree because ... Disagree because ... A little bit of both because ...

_____

_____

_____

_____

_____

3. A man should provide for his family.

Agree because ... Disagree because ... A little bit of both because ...

_____

_____

_____

_____

_____

4. The kids should always come first.

Agree because ... Disagree because ... A little bit of both because ...

_____

_____

_____

5. Find an activity you can do together.

Agree because ... Disagree because ... A little bit of both because ...

_____

_____

_____

_____

6. Always maintain separate social lives, at least to some extent.

Agree because ... Disagree because ... A little bit of both because ...

_____

_____

_____

_____

7. You should feel comfortable sharing e-mail passwords with your partner because you both shouldn't have anything to hide.

Agree because ... Disagree because ... A little bit of both because ...

_____

_____

_____

_____

_____

8. Treat your partner's family like your own.

Agree because ... Disagree because ... A little bit of both because ...

_____

_____

_____

9. Never say anything negative about your partner to other people.

Agree because ... Disagree because ... A little bit of both because ...

_____

_____

_____

_____

10. You should tell your partner everything.

Agree because ... Disagree because ... A little bit of both because ...

_____

_____

_____

_____

LET'S HEAR YOUR CONFESSIONS

1. Have you ever violated someone's trust?

   _____

   _____

   _____

2. What's the worst thing you've done to gain acceptance from a person or group?

   _____

   _____

   _____

3. Have you ever lied to get something you wanted?

   _____

   _____

   _____

4. Have you ever committed a crime?

   _____

   _____

   _____

5. Have you ever considered getting a tattoo?

   _____

   _____

   _____

6. Have you ever stolen anything?

_____

_____

_____

7. What's the worst thing you think you've ever done?

_____

_____

_____

8. Have you ever taken recreational drugs?

_____

_____

_____

9. Have you ever wondered if you have a problem with alcohol?

_____

_____

_____

10. Have you ever been in a physical fight?

_____

_____

_____

11. Have you ever had a sexual encounter with someone who was married?

_____

_____

_____

WHAT ARE OUR RELATIONSHIP FORTES?

1. Who's more romantic? Me ❏ | You ❏

2. Who's more thoughtful? Me ❏ | You ❏

3. Who's better at listening when one of us has had a bad day? Me ❏ | You ❏

4. Who's better at calming the other one down? Me ❏ | You ❏

5. Who's better at setting the mood? Me ❏ | You ❏

6. Who's better at defusing a fight? Me ❏ | You ❏

7. Who's better at taking care of the other person when he or she is sick? Me ❏ | You ❏

8. Who's better at celebrating the other person's accomplishments? Me ❏ | You ❏

9. Who's more reliable? Me ❏ | You ❏

10. Who gives a better massage? Me ❏ | You ❏

THOSE GOLDEN DAYS
OF CHILDHOOD

1. What was your craziest childhood injury?

_____

_____

_____

2. What game did you most love to play as a kid?

_____

_____

_____

3. What's the most embarrassing thing that happened to you as a child? (Something you can't even think about now without blushing.)

_____

_____

_____

4. What's the most humiliating thing that happened to you as a teenager?

_____

_____

_____

5. When you were five years old, what did you want to be when you grew up?

_____

_____

_____

You   Me
You   Me
You   Me
You   Me
You   Me
You   Me
You   Me
WOULD YOU RATHER?

6. When you were fifteen, what did you think you'd be when you're the age you are now?

_____

_____

_____

7. Who was your biggest childhood crush in the world of television or movies?

_____

_____

_____

8. Who was someone you admired when you were a child, other than your mother and father? (We're assuming you admired them.)

_____

_____

_____

9. What movie or TV show could you not live without as a kid?

_____

_____

_____

10. As a child, what did you get in trouble for most often?

_____

_____

_____

11. As a kid, where was your special hiding place, where you could be alone and shut out the rest of the world?

_____

_____

Skydive or bungee jump? * Become president or become
alty? * Buy a huge ... or your own a private island? * Inv
something that changes the world or win the lottery? * Cl
Mon... ... ... Great Blue Hole in Bel
* Pu... ... a hit song? * Go to C
nival in Rio or do running with the bulls in Spain? * Join

CELEBRATING
THE HOLIDAYS

1. How do you feel about celebrating holidays?

_____

_____

_____

2. Do you have a favorite holiday?

_____

_____

_____

3. Do you have a least favorite holiday?

_____

_____

_____

4. What's your favorite holiday tradition?

_____

_____

_____

5. What's your favorite holiday food?

_____

_____

_____

WOULD YOU RATHER?
Skydive or bungee jump? * Become president or become
something that changes the world or win the lottery? * Cl
Mount Everest or scuba-dive the Great Blue Hole in Bel
* Publish a bestselling book or write a hit song? * Go to C
nival in Rio or do running with the bulls in Spain? * Join

6. Were holidays important to your family when you were growing up?

_____

_____

_____

7. How have holiday celebrations changed as you've gotten older?

_____

_____

_____

8. Is there anything you dread about the holidays?

_____

_____

_____

9. Do you prefer to spend the holidays with your whole family, or just your immediate family?

_____

_____

_____

10. What's the most important holiday tradition you'd like to continue with your own children?

_____

_____

_____

OUR CAREER GOALS

1. What's your ultimate goal for your career?

_____

_____

_____

2. What kind of support do you need from me to accomplish this?

_____

_____

_____

3. How do you think we can better support each other's career on a regular basis?

_____

_____

_____

4. Do you think we have compatible work ethics?

_____

_____

_____

5. What do you envision me doing other than my current job?

_____

_____

_____

6. What advice do you have for me based on what you know about my career goals?

_____

_____

_____

7. How would you feel if I wanted to give up my career when we have kids?

_____

_____

_____

8. Would you be willing to relocate if you got an incredible career opportunity?

_____

_____

_____

9. Would you be willing to relocate if I got an incredible career opportunity?

_____

_____

_____

10. What advice would you give me if I hated my job and wanted to quit?

_____

_____

_____

11. What's more important: having a job that's lucrative, or having a job that you love?

_____

_____

Skydive or bungee jump? * Become president or become r
alty? * Buy a huge ... ch or your own a private island? * Inv
something that changes the world or win the lottery? * Cli
Mou ... Great Blue Hole in Beli
* Publish a ... el or write a hit song? * Go to C
nival in Rio or do running with the bulls in Spain? * Join ...

YOUR TALENTS
AS A KID

1. Did your parents encourage you (or make you) play a musical instrument?

_____

_____

_____

2. What sports did you play when you were young?

_____

_____

_____

3. Did you take any other classes, like dance or karate?

_____

_____

_____

4. For what did you show a talent or aptitude as a kid?

_____

_____

_____

5. Did you ever do any child modeling or beauty pageants?

_____

_____

_____

6. Were you in any accelerated classes?

_____

_____

_____

7. Which school clubs did you join?

_____

_____

_____

8. Did you compete in (or win) any big competitions or contests?

_____

_____

_____

9. Were you ever featured on TV or in a magazine?

_____

_____

_____

10. Was there ever any sibling rivalry over who was better at what?

_____

_____

_____

WHAT ADVICE WILL YOU
GIVE YOUR KIDS...

1. When they are starting kindergarten?

_____

_____

_____

_____

2. When they start going through puberty?

_____

_____

_____

_____

3. On their first day of high school?

_____

_____

_____

_____

4. When they start applying to college?

_____

_____

_____

_____

5. At their college graduation?

_____

_____

6. After their first heartbreak?

_____

_____

_____

7. On their wedding day?

_____

_____

_____

8. When they have kids?

_____

_____

_____

9. If they are fired from a job?

_____

_____

_____

10. If they want to change career paths?

_____

_____

_____

WOULD YOU RATHER?
Skydive or bungee jump? * Become president or become r...
...ty? * Buy a huge ranch or your own a private island? * Inv...
something that changes the world or win the lottery? * Cli...
...in Beli...
Publish a bestselling book or write a hit song? * Go to C...
...val in Rio or do running with the bulls in Spain? * Join...

WHAT'S ON YOUR BUCKET LIST?

Skydive — **Me** ❑ | **You** ❑

Bungee jump — **Me** ❑ | **You** ❑

Buy a ranch — **Me** ❑ | **You** ❑

Retire on your own private island — **Me** ❑ | **You** ❑

Invent something that changes the world — **Me** ❑ | **You** ❑

Win the lottery — **Me** ❑ | **You** ❑

Climb Mount Everest — **Me** ❑ | **You** ❑

Scuba-dive the Great Blue Hole in Belize — **Me** ❑ | **You** ❑

Write your life story — **Me** ❑ | **You** ❑

Go to Carnival in Rio — **Me** ❑ | **You** ❑

Run with the bulls in Spain — **Me** ❑ | **You** ❑

Set a world record — **Me** ❑ | **You** ❑

Join Teach for America — **Me** ❑ | **You** ❑

Learn how to fly a plane — **Me** ❑ | **You** ❑

Live on a lake — **Me** ❑ | **You** ❑

Visit every continent — **Me** ❑ | **You** ❑

Visit every state — **Me** ❑ | **You** ❑

Be on a reality TV show — **Me** ❑ | **You** ❑

CHOOSING
YOUR RELIGION

1. What role does religion currently play in your life?

_____

_____

_____

2. What role did religion play in your life when you were growing up?

_____

_____

_____

3. How has your view of religion changed over time, if at all?

_____

_____

_____

4. What do you think the purpose of religion is, in the philosophical sense?

_____

_____

_____

5. Do you feel that religion has had a positive or negative influence on you?

_____

_____

_____

WOULD YOU RATHER?

Skydive or bungee jump? * Become president or become
something that changes the world or win the lottery? * C
Mount Everest or scuba-dive the Great Blue Hole in Be
* Publish a bestselling book or write a hit song? * Go to
nival in Rio or do running with the bulls in Spain? * Join

6. In general, do you think religion influences people for better or
for worse?

_____

_____

_____

7. Is it important for you to share your life with someone of the same
religious background?

_____

_____

_____

8. Do you feel that certain religions are better, or are more credible,
than others?

_____

_____

_____

9. How important is it that you raise your children in a certain faith?

_____

_____

_____

10. How would you feel if I wanted to change my religious beliefs, or
convert to another faith?

_____

_____

_____

HOW DO YOU PREFER
TO SPEND YOUR WEEKEND?

1. Sleep in or wake up early? Me _____ You _____

2. Work out or veg out? Me _____ You _____

3. Run errands or relax? Me _____ You _____

4. Cook at home or eat out? Me _____ You _____

5. Mini-vacation or enjoy time
   at home? Me _____ You _____

6. Work on the house/chores or
   just do fun stuff? Me _____ You _____

7. See friends and family or be
   a homebody? Me _____ You _____

8. Be active outside or shop/see movies? Me _____ You _____

9. Hit the town all dressed up or stay
   in your PJs as much as possible? Me _____ You _____

10. Read a book or complete a
    creative project? Me _____ You _____

YOUR LEGACY

1. What do you want your legacy to be?

_____

_____

_____

2. If you could be known for one thing, what would it be?

_____

_____

_____

3. What is the one thing you must accomplish in your lifetime?

_____

_____

_____

4. If today was your last day on Earth, what would be your biggest regret?

_____

_____

_____

5. What do you think the meaning of life is?

_____

_____

_____

6. If you were put on Earth for a reason, what reason was it?

7. If I outlive you, what do you want me to remember about you when you're gone?

_____

_____

_____

8. What lasting impression would you hope to leave on your kids when you're gone?

_____

_____

_____

9. If you were to die tomorrow, what about your life or your accomplishments would you be most proud of?

_____

_____

_____

10. Would you rather be remembered fondly for fifty years or notoriously for 5,000 years?

_____

_____

_____

WOULD YOU RATHER?
Skydive or bungee jump? Become president or become
alry? Buy a huge ranch or your own a private island? Inv
something that changes the world or win the lottery? Cli
Mou... Great Blue Hole in Beli
...hit song? Go to C
...nival in Rio or do running with the bulls in Spain? Join

PIE-IN-THE-SKY ACCOMPLISHMENTS

1. If you were to write a book, what would it be about?

_____

_____

_____

2. If you were to make a movie, what genre would it be?

_____

_____

_____

3. If you were to donate money to a school, what would it be for?

_____

_____

_____

4. If you were to create a TV show, what kind of show would it be?

_____

_____

_____

5. If you were going to open a restaurant, what kind of cuisine would it have?

_____

_____

_____

6. If you were going to open a bar, what would it be like?

_____

_____

7. If you were going to invent something revolutionary, how would it change the world?

_____

_____

8. If you could buy a yacht, what would you name it?

_____

_____

9. If you could open a theme park, what attractions would it have?

_____

_____

10. If you were to invent a new soda or snack food, what would it be?

_____

_____

11. If you were a rock star, what would your band or stage name be?

_____

_____

12. If you were a sports icon, how would you pose on the Wheaties box?

_____

_____

END OF LIFE STUFF...
SORRY TO BE A DOWNER

1. Would you prefer to go to a nursing home or have an at-home nurse?

_____
_____
_____

2. Would you prefer a burial or cremation?

_____
_____
_____

3. Do you think it's better to die instantly or gradually?

_____
_____
_____

4. Would you prefer to pass away in your sleep or consciously?

_____
_____
_____

5. Would you prefer to pass away before me or after me?

_____
_____
_____

6. Would you prefer to know you have a terminal illness or die never knowing?

_____

_____

_____

7. What are your thoughts about having a funeral?

_____

_____

_____

8. Do you have a will or plan on writing one at some point?

_____

_____

_____

9. Would you want to be put on life support?

_____

_____

_____

10. If you were to have a tombstone, what would you want it to say?

_____

_____

_____

11. Who would you want beside you when you're on your deathbed?

_____

_____

_____

WOULD YOU RATHER?

Skydive or bungee jump? * Become president or become ~~~~~~
~~~~? * Buy a huge ~~~~~ or your own a private island? * Inv~~
something that changes the world or win the lottery? * Ch~~
M~~~~~ ~~~~~~~~~~~~~~~~ ~~~~~at Blue Hole in Bel~~
* Publish ~~~~~~~~~~~~~ or write a hit song? * Go to C~~
nival in Rio or do running with the bulls in Spain? * Join ~

ANOTHER BUNCH
OF FIRSTS

1. Where's the first place you went to outside of your hometown?

_____

_____

_____

2. Who was your first teacher that you really remember?

_____

_____

_____

3. Who was your first best friend?

_____

_____

_____

4. When's the first time you drove a car?

_____

_____

_____

5. When did you have your first alcoholic drink?

_____

_____

_____

WOULD YOU RATHER?

Skydive or bungee jump? * Become president or become
own a private island? * In
something that changes the world or win the lottery? * C
Mount Everest or scuba-dive the Great Blue Hole in Be
* Publish a bestselling book or write a hit song? * Go to
nival in Rio or do running with the bulls in Spain? * Join

6. When was the first time you traveled on a plane?

_____

_____

_____

7. What's the first restaurant you remember eating at?

_____

_____

_____

8. What's the first movie you remember seeing?

_____

_____

_____

9. What's the first song that moved you?

_____

_____

_____

10. What was your first school dance like?

_____

_____

_____

WHAT ARE YOUR DEEPEST, DARKEST FEARS AND WILDEST DREAMS?

1. What scares you most in life?

    _____

    _____

    _____

2. What keeps you from fulfilling your dreams?

    _____

    _____

    _____

3. What would you do with your life if you knew you were guaranteed to succeed?

    _____

    _____

    _____

4. In what way do you tend to doubt yourself the most?

    _____

    _____

    _____

5. What worries you most about the future?

    _____

    _____

    _____

You   Me

You   Me

You   Me

You   Me

You   Me

You   Me

You   Me

6. How do you think fear holds you back?

_____

_____

_____

7. What scares you the most about our relationship?

_____

_____

_____

8. What hypothetical future event do you think you fear the most?

_____

_____

_____

9. How would you feel if you grew old without accomplishing your dreams?

_____

_____

_____

10. What would it take for you to give up on a dream?

_____

_____

_____

WOULD YOU RATHER?

Skydive or bungee jump? Become president or become
... Buy a huge ... or your own a private island? In...
something that changes the world or win the lottery? Cl...
... Great ... little in Bel...
... a hit single? Go to C...
... to Rio or do running with the bulls in Spain? Join...

YOU FINISHED
THE BOOK QUIZ!

1. How do you feel about our relationship after completing this book?

_____

_____

_____

2. What's the most surprising thing you shared with me?

_____

_____

_____

3. What's the most surprising thing I shared with you?

_____

_____

_____

4. Were there any questions you really didn't want to answer, or were tempted to skip?

_____

_____

_____

5. What's the most important thing you learned about me that you didn't know before?

_____

_____

_____

6. What do you think you learned about yourself?

_____

_____

_____

7. Do you think there is anything we can change or work on in our relationship after going through these quizzes?

_____

_____

_____

8. Has your opinion or view of me changed at all after listening to my answers?

_____

_____

_____

9. How do you think we can improve our communication skills moving forward?

_____

_____

_____

10. How did these quizzes help you appreciate me (or our relationship) more than you already do?

_____

_____

_____

ABOUT THE AUTHOR

Natasha Burton is a journalist and relationships expert who blogs for Cosmopolitan.com and is a regular contributor to *Maxim*, Glo.com, MSN, WomansDay.com, iVillage, and Mom.me. She's also the coauthor of *The Little Black Book of Big Red Flags* (Adams Media, 2011), a critically acclaimed dating guide that has been translated into multiple languages.

Burton holds a master's degree in creative writing from the University of Southern California, where she formerly taught composition. She lives in Santa Barbara, California, with her fiancé, who graciously encourages her to write about their love life when the occasion calls for it. Which . . . turns out to be almost every day.